MISUNDERSTOOD

MISUNDERSTOOD

By Anne Jobes

PEN PUBLISHING

Jobes, Anne, 2010
    Misunderstood, First Edition, December 2010
ISBN 1456405950 (soft cover), EAN-13 is 978-1456405953,
Book # 3512746

1.   Self-help, empathy, awareness, understanding

LIBRARY OF CONGRESS CATALOGING-IN-
PUBLICATION DATA

*I was mistaken in believing that I
could give anyone anything other
than what I want for myself.
Since I want to experience peace,
Love and forgiveness, these are
the only gifts I would offer others.
It is not charity on my part to offer
forgiveness and Love to others in
place of attack. Rather, offering
Love is the only way I can accept
Love for myself.*

-Gerald G. Jampolsky, M.D.

Acknowledgements

I would like to thank my daughter, Sydney for reading this book and assisting me in the editing process.

I would also like to thank the many people in my life that I have misunderstood and who have misunderstood me.

Lastly, I would like to thank my friend, Peter, for helping me to realize the importance of "intent," "first thought," and in understanding the meaning of Divine Love.

Misunderstood

WATCH WHAT YOU THINK,

IT BECOMES WHAT YOU SAY.

WATCH WHAT YOU SAY,

IT BECOMES WHAT YOU DO.

WATCH WHAT YOU DO,

IT BECOMES YOUR CHARACTER.

WATCH YOUR CHARACTER,

IT DETERMINES WHAT YOUR FUTURE WILL BE
LIKE...

Table of Contents

Introduction   page 15

Chapter One –Evolutionary
          Awareness   page 21

Chapter Two – Sally   page 27

Chapter Three - Subdivisions upon
          Subdivisions   page 33

Chapter Four - Don't Judge a Man
          Until You Have Walked Two
          Moons in His Moccasins…
                                        page 35

Chapter Five - Emotional Fight or
          Flight   page 39

Chapter Six – Kathy   page 51

Chapter Seven - A Human
          Experience   page 57

Chapter Eight - Consciously Kind
                                        page 61

A Perfect Seed   page 65

Introduction

It's easy to understand why someone doesn't understand you.

How could they, after all? They aren't you. **Empathy is an option of consciousness**. How can anyone comprehend how you feel or why you do the things you do? How can *you* realize *their* choices or emotions?

It may well be that what we consider to be **true empathy is nothing more than benevolent guesswork**. We can only see someone's point of view or expression of emotion from a vantage point that is less than perfect – our own. It's like living on a mountain all your life, having the perfect view of a sunset over the valley below. But from the valley, the vision is a very different thing. It's the same sunset, of course, but if we've never been atop that mountain we cannot truly understand the vastness of color that spreads across the universal sky. If we have never been embraced within the valley we can never know the softness of color as it sinks over the surrounding trees and rising land.

We cannot know what it is like to be black if we are white. We cannot know what it is like to be rich if we are poor. We cannot know the pain of losing a child if we've never had a child. All of this may be obvious; however more subtle truths can be more complex to comprehend. In fact, **judgment is created in the assumption that you are the only one who knows what "right" is *and* that you know how someone else should act**.

We roll our eyes at people who talk to themselves, who are overweight or drink themselves into oblivion. We think we know how other people should spend their money, discipline their children or act within their faith. Heck, we even think we know what kind of faith other people should have!

I know quite a few people who see what others do and say things like, "*I understand that they've gone through things, but there comes a time when they have to take responsibility for (whatever it is)*." Or I hear, "*If you don't like something about yourself, just change it. Just stop doing the things you don't like*." Naturally, there is a deep wisdom in the proposal that being accountable for our actions and choices makes sense. I don't think anyone doubts that we can make changes in our lives that can help create a consciousness for security, happiness and growth. But what does all of that really mean if we can't or don't see the source of our impulses? And *why* are we blind to our own motivation yet so able to clearly see what everyone else is doing wrong?

This is a book about empathy. My inspiration for writing it was born in the desire to be understood. I can't say that I have any altruistic ideas about helping anyone. I probably just want to delicately complain. If I am honest with myself, I'm probably even having a marvelous pity party with myself as I point out the wisdom of attempting to attain compassion.

I have no degree in psychology. Nor am I a professional social worker. I am not a graduate of a theological institution. I am a 56-year-old woman who has, for whatever reason, always attempted to understand the people around me by stepping gently into their shoes (though they never really fit). I've tried to stand in their perspective –

even if they lived on the mountain and
I lived in the valley.

These are my thoughts...

Self importance is our greatest enemy. Think about it - what weakens us is feeling offended by the deeds and misdeeds of our fellowmen. Our self importance requires that we spend most of our lives offended by someone.

-Carlos Castaneda

Chapter One
Evolutionary Awareness

I believe that there are only two things going on in the human psyche: positive and negative experiences. These can further (and more easily) be broken down to Love and Fear experiences. This is not a new concept, of course. World renowned author and teacher, Gerald G. Jampolsky[1] has written about this model in many wonderful books.

What brings us to experience Love more clearly than Fear (in my opinion) seems to have more to do with evolution than conscious choice most of the time. It is, interestingly, the choice to act in Love rather than Fear that probably causes the evolution.

---

[1] Gerald G. Jampolsky, M.D., a child and adult psychiatrist, is a graduate of Stanford Medical School. In 1975, he founded the first Center for Attitudinal Healing, now a worldwide network with independent centers in over thirty countries. He is an internationally recognized authority in the fields of psychiatry, health, business, and education. Dr. Jampolsky has published extensively, including his best-selling Love Is Letting Go of Fear. He and his wife, psychotherapist and author Diane Cirincione, Ph.D., have worked in forty-nine countries and currently reside in both northern California and Hawaii.

And so, it becomes a circle of evolutionary awareness.

Consciousness is described by *Answers.com* as *"A sense of one's personal or collective identity, including the attitudes, beliefs, and sensitivities held by or considered characteristic of an individual or group."* It's obvious that consciousness is something that is deeply imbedded into our approach to life – personally and professionally. Our consciousness can be considered political, racial or religious. It can be inspired by family, country and age (as well as many other separating forces).

It is, on a more foundational level, AWARENESS that brings about the most significant changes in our lives. Becoming aware of our own actions, feelings and choices can only happen if we first become responsive to our own thoughts (and the possibility that something and/or someone molded those thoughts). This is probably the purpose of psychology. Psychology is described as the science of the mind or of mental states and processes. We go to a psychologist or therapist to try to sort out the details of our lives so that we can let go of some of our fear and learn, not only forgiveness, but how to love ourselves. It's a worthy process.

Perhaps just as meaningful, however, is the process of spiritual growth - being aware that our attitudes, our thoughts and our inner strengths (or weaknesses) may be handed to us from a deeper level of ourselves than that which can be explained physically or psychologically. Letting go of Fear may have more to do with the acceptance of Love than anything else. That's the part that's tricky. Most of us want to be loved. We want to love. But we don't really accept what it is or what that means.

Believe me, I'm no expert here. I'll be the first one to admit that there have been many times in my life when I haven't felt loved (on a human level). I'm not sure I completely believe that most of the people in my life actually love ME (emphasis on "me"). I accept as true that they think they do. I suppose that on a very human level they feel a requirement to love me because of my place in their lives. I'm a Mom. My children have no valid choice but to love me. I'm a wife. My husband thinks he loves me. I have friends. They feel something akin to love in many cases. I'm not sure I believe that most of them actually love me unconditionally or without expectation. Maybe this same insecurity is at the root of most people's misunderstanding of other people. It's not a good feeling. In fact, being misunderstood often feels like you aren't liked.

I personally have felt misunderstood more often than not. I can't say why that happens but I'm sure my suspicions of not being loved are rooted in my experiences of being misunderstood.

So why does it feel so bad to be misunderstood? Why do we get frustrated and angry if someone misunderstands us? It often times does make us feel sad.

It's all about acceptance; that is – being accepted. No matter how secure we think we are; no matter how well-adjusted or strong-willed we are, it can feel very much like we are not being respected, listened to or paid attention to when someone misunderstands our words, actions or expressions of emotion.

It hits to the core of our being and creates a space of disconnect. This can happen in the most mundane or superficial associations as well as the more important, closer relationships of our lives. Whether we want to admit it or not – we care. We care about what people think. If we didn't, we wouldn't get angry. We wouldn't feel sad. We wouldn't get defensive.

So what can we do about those feelings when they arise? Once again, they are deeply rooted in the human psyche – the human experience. Can we really change how we innately react to someone else's judgment of us? Can we allow them their misunderstanding without feeling negative responses within?

Perhaps not. But if it *is* possible, it will only happen if we begin to try to understand that we cannot understand anyone else; and they will never really be able to understand us. We can't take it personally. It really has nothing to do with US or our worth.

The most important purpose of these negative feelings that we experience when someone misunderstands us, is that they serve as a reminder that we are also capable of making someone else feel the same way – frustrated – angry or sad. We CAN control our own actions, thoughts and words so that we are not bringing these feelings to the surface within others.

What a gift it is to know that we can deter distressing feelings! This, in and of itself, is a true expression of acceptance.

Chapter Two
Sally

Sally is a twenty-three year old woman who gets easily annoyed at the people she works with. She finds things like their faces, their voices, their little personality quirks to be more than she can stand sometimes. She finds their choices of entertainment to be stupid and a waste of time. She is short-tempered and quick to judge when she's around them.

Sally is also judgmental with her family members.

If one would ask Sally why she feels this way, her answer would be something like, "*People have got to stop blaming their present on their past. You are who you are. If something's not working, just fix it. I can't stand when people aren't responsible for what they do,*" or "*She's weird. I can't stand her or the way she walks and talks. I can't even look at her.*" (Referring, for instance to one of her co-workers). She might say more than that!

The things that she feels (from her point of view) are not completely irrational. They make perfect sense. She realizes that she's judgmental but also believes that her judgments are sound and reasonable – that they have merit.

There are four things going on as you read this: 1) Sally's point of view, 2) Our opinion about Sally's point of view, 3) Our ability to understand why Sally feels what she feels, and 4) Sally's understanding of why she feels what she feels.

Sally's point of view comes from what she feels; and what she feels is born in the experiences of her life, her personality and her most inner awareness of these things.

Most of us could look at Sally, listen to her and decide from our own viewpoint if what she's feeling or if the way she is acting is valid. Most of us would easily find something wrong with her attitude.

Truly empathizing with her would mean that we'd have to honor why she feels the way she feels (even if we have no idea of the "why"). We'd have to be open minded enough to open our hearts to her. We all have that capability but do it, as you would expect, on many different levels.

The final and probably most important thing is Sally's ability to become conscious of why she feels what she feels. This is where true awareness is born. And this is also where change begins.

Whew! With all of that going on it's no wonder that communication, compassion and understanding between human beings seems so difficult!

But the next question is: is that a good thing or a bad thing? And where does Love fit into the whole thing?

If we consider Sally and her attitude toward others we can easily see that she is a person who feels a pressing need to raise herself up above others. Is Sally aware of this need or does she truly believe that she *is* better than others?

Chances are good that if she truly believes herself to be better than other people, her psychological need to raise herself up is also very real.

Interestingly, if she were actually aware of the need, she would be on the long journey of self-reflection and eventually, empathy. It's obvious that Sally hasn't yet Googled© that map.

So, what is it that creates the fertile ground for personal growth from the inside out?

In order for human beings to reach to their own divine selves, there must be a willingness to discover something within their deepest nature - to recognize the possibility of their purpose and be aware of their own essence. This means that we must accept the human condition, be aware of our true philosophy and be willing to understand that we are part of a greater energy than ourselves.

It seems like some people are uniquely predisposed to lofty thoughts about spirit – heaven and earth, and the growth of Soul. It's also quite obvious that others do not consider these things at all. There are many more people who talk about it but don't act in it (probably most of us).

So what is it that makes us all see even the most fundamental things so very differently?

Chapter Three
Subdivisions upon Subdivisions

There are dozens upon dozens of things that separate us – make us different (unique) and special. A few of those things include:

- Gender
- Sexual preference
- Family placement
- Religion
- Neighborhood
- Family size
- Financial stability
- City/State/Country
- School/teachers
- Natural talents/interests
- Vocation
- Training
- Temperament
- Friends/acquaintances
- Race
- Nationality
- Intelligence
- Physical ability
- Traditions
- Experiences
- Emotions
- Childhood rearing
- Education
- Reasoning ability
- Instincts

Let's face it; the list could probably go on and on! Each one of these things (and the things I may have missed) has subdivisions upon subdivisions and each of these differences create differences in us.

It really is overwhelming.

So, where do we begin to understand all of this? How can we find empathy with one another – acceptance of these differences instead of frustration, judgment and separation? The bottom line is: How can we accept and care for one another?

It all begins with our own understanding of us.

Chapter Four
Don't Judge a Man Until You Have Walked Two Moons in His Moccasins...

Imagine yourself born into a home of Native Americans living in Montana. Do you know that there are twenty different Native American tribes in the state of Montana? Twenty different expressions of one culture of people. Within just one of those tribes there are hundreds of extended families. Each extended family may have anywhere from one to seventy members (or more). Each extended family is made up of many individual families. Each individual family is made up of very different people.

The potential for differentiation with each of these people is endless. Just because they are Native American, live in the same state and belong to the same tribe does not mean that they are the same. There are men and women, first born – last born, richer – poorer, doctors, supermarket workers and farmers. Some of these people were raised more traditionally as their culture might demand, others were raised more Americanized. Some finished high school – some dropped out.

Just like you and I, we are created within the life we lead. Our personalities and temperaments are molded and nurtured by the scenery we develop within. We learn patience or intolerance by example. We learn how to love ourselves by how worthy we are meant to feel.

According the 1995 US Census there are between 1754 and 1763 different Native American tribes in the United States and Canada. To understand just ONE culture (which is only ONE thing that creates individuality) is an obviously impossible task.

Generally, we can assume a lot about the Native American culture – the traditions that we know about, the spirituality that we've been made aware of, the iniquitous treatment they've endured and the warmth of their closeness. But these universal qualities might fit any culture: black, brown, yellow, white or red. If we are to understand or find empathy with someone else, the first thing to realize is that we can NEVER know what they feel or why they feel it. We can NEVER know the choices that they are aware of or the consciousness they live within. We can NEVER really stand (let alone walk) in their shoes.

So, is empathy impossible? I don't think so. I think it's an attainable goal that cannot be reached within the constraints of human experience. It is a quest of Soul. It is about who WE are – not about who someone else seems to be.

But *where* do we start?

Chapter Five
Emotional Fight or Flight

Let's revisit Sally. What is it about other people that so easily gets on Sally's nerves? Is she really surrounded by incompetent idiots? I suppose it's possible...

It's more likely that the people whom Sally believes are ugly, stupid, disrespectful and weird are all loved by someone. They are somebody's child, sister, father or spouse. They have lives unlike anything Sally can imagine. They have physical strengths and restraints that are different than hers. They have a religion she can't understand. They have a history she cannot begin to relate to. Each one of them is a unique person – like Sally – just as important – just as special – just as worthy of love.

So what's with Sally? Why can't she see it? Or perhaps the better question is: why can't she act in it?

If we asked Sally about her judgments she would probably agree that she has oftentimes been disparaging to people. She would probably also agree that everyone deserves to be loved and respected. Her natural self – her true self – her inner self is aware of kindness, empathy and acceptance. The idea that she's a bad person is, of course, ridiculous. How many of us (if any) are truly 'bad' people? I have a notion that none of us are. But I *do* believe that we have negative thoughts and choose to act in those pessimistic deliberations by creating and then perpetuating a sense of grandeur for ourselves. In other words, we're terrified of not being loved and our reaction to that fear is rather like a fight or flight response that is emotionally based.

The physiologic fight or flight response is a *fundamental physical response and is our body's primitive, automatic, inborn response that prepares the body to "fight" or "flee" from perceived attack, harm or threat to our survival.*

What happens to us when we are under excessive stress?

When we experience excessive stress—whether from internal worry or external circumstance—a bodily reaction is triggered, called the "fight or flight" response. Originally discovered

*by the great Harvard physiologist
Walter Cannon, this response is hard-
wired into our brains and represents a
genetic wisdom designed to protect us
from bodily harm. This response
actually corresponds to an area of our
brain called the hypothalamus, which—
when stimulated—initiates a sequence
of nerve cell firing and chemical release
that prepares our body for running or
fighting.*[2]

So what would "emotional" fight
or flight be? Obviously, physiologic
fight or flight is a natural, ancient
response that is involuntarily innate.
We don't think about it – it just
happens.

Would "emotional" fight or flight
be the same? Is it involuntary? Is it
natural? Why do some people take
things personally while others let
things slide off their back – or better
yet – they don't even notice them?

Maybe it starts at birth. Maybe it
starts before that. One thing that's

---

2 Neil F. Neimark, M.D

certain is that we all respond to emotional stimuli and stress more often than physical reactions of fear.

Considering Sally, let's assume that she was raised in a family of five. She is the youngest of three children. Her mother and father were high school sweethearts and married after quite a long courtship. Both of her parents came from somewhat dysfunctional homes where neither of them was made to feel accepted for who they were. Their parenting skills were not polished by the experience of having been raised by people who were good examples of parenting.

Sally's older brother is a typical boy but is extraordinarily criticized by his father and smothered by his mother. Her bother's personality is rounded by intelligence, playfulness and sensitivity.

Sally's older sister is a very typical little girl – frills, dolls and playing school are some of the things that attract her as she's growing up. She is, however, self-reliant and a bit bossy. She has a quick temper (like her father) and enjoys being in charge of Sally while pretending to be more grown up like her brother.

Sally is quiet as a child. Her natural Moro Reflex[3] as an infant is more apparent than is typical. She seems content most of the time – rarely crying, though she is very observant. She doesn't really react very much to her surroundings as she gets older. She seems to be quietly swallowing her experiences. Separation anxiety[4] is

---

[3] This odd fear of falling is known as the Moro reflex (also known as the 'startle reflex'). It is present in newborns but usually disappears within a few months. At birth, the pediatrician will test the baby for this reflex by laying her down on her back and removing contact with her. She is expected to throw her arms and legs out and extend her head in fear. Sometimes the doctor will also test the baby with a sudden loud noise, which should result in a similar reaction. Watching a baby experience the Moro reflex is almost comical, as you have to wonder what could be so alarming that she would feel like she's falling, and appear to grab on to thin air for dear life. In actual fact, the baby is experiencing a kind of sensation that she is all alone in the world for a split second, and her reaction (instantaneously grabbing for something to hold on to) is a protective mechanism, akin to the 'fight or flight' response. –**Baby Slumber.com**

[4] Sometime between 4-7 months, babies develop a sense of object permanence and begin to learn that things and people exist even when they're out of sight. This is when babies start playing the "dropsy" game — dropping things over the side of the high chair and expecting an adult to retrieve it (which, once retrieved, gets dropped again!). The same thing occurs with a parent. Babies realize that there's only mom or dad, and when they can't see you, that means you've gone away. And most don't yet understand the concept of time so do not know if or when you'll come back. Whether you're in the kitchen, in the next bedroom, or at the office, it's all the same to your baby. You've disappeared, and your child will do whatever he or she can to prevent this from happening. -**Kids Health**

intense for her and lasts well into her early school years – long after most children have outgrown it.

As Sally gets older and her sister begins hanging out with friends that don't include Sally, Sally's feeling of rejection is obvious. Instead of crying, however, she gets angry. She begins to negatively judge her sister's choices. The same is true for her brother who has begun a tumultuous emotional tumble as his self-esteem plummets as an older teen. Sally's reaction to their actions is very telling of the complete fear that has been suppressed for so many years.

Fear has many faces. Any negative emotion has a foundation of fear. There are a couple of hormones related to fear: Cortisol and Norepinephrine. Stress hormones act by mobilizing energy from storage to muscles, increasing heart rate, blood pressure and breathing rate and shutting down metabolic processes such as digestion, reproduction, growth and immunity.

Constant (including low-lying or subtle) stress causes continual release of stress hormones which causes:

- A depletion of energy storage
- High blood pressure
- Stress-induced hypertension
- Affects on metabolic processes
- Ulcers (digestion)
- Hampers growth
- Decrease in testosterone levels in males and irregular menstrual cycles in females.
- Increases likelihood of infectious diseases.[5]

When stress becomes chronic, lasting for long periods of time without any moments of rest or relaxation, serious physical or psychological problems can result. Some of these include:

- Anxiety or Depressive Disorder
- Heart Disease and Stroke
- Weight
- Sleep Difficulty
- Concentration and Memory
- Pain
- Gastrointestinal Disorders

After being born with a more fearful temperament and quiet personality, Sally has watched her brother's abuse, her mother's fear

---

[5] Wikipedia®

and her sister's bid for power. Sally felt like the odd man out. She pushed everything deep inside and for whatever reasons, did not express anything to anyone. Now that she's feeling abandoned by her siblings and still holding fear because of the abuse she has watched, she begins to have unexplained pain. Her stomach hurts. She's afraid of throwing up. She pulls further into herself and the more introverted she becomes, the more judgmental she becomes. She is certain she has a terrible disease that the doctors haven't discovered.

The disease is fear.

As she gets older, grows and has a couple of close personal relationships with men, she begins to feel more independent. She attains employment where she succeeds and moves ahead quickly. She becomes financially stable and begins to feel pride in her accomplishments. Her self-confidence grows.

But somewhere beneath the surface, something else is growing too. It surfaces in a need to be in control of something she has never faced. Her sense of being right – of doing things right – of making the right decisions (compared to other people who have – in her mind – made the wrong decisions) develops more acutely. Her judgments – so obviously born in her fear of rejection and feelings of danger – have become so intense that she seems to find no positives in anything that have surrounded her and supported her during her lifetime. Her country, her culture, her family, and her acquaintances – these have all become things she finds error and lack of trust with. The only person who does not quite fall into this category is the one person who (as a child) she probably feared most – her father. Instead of accepting his bad choices, she embraces them as "normal." It's a way of denying the 'raison d'être' (reason for her fear). If the reason doesn't exist – then her fear doesn't exist either.

She's in complete denial within her own supremacy.

It's a comfortable place to be as long as she never has to act or react because of her inner fear. And that's where the problem lies. We don't have a choice with that. We can't help but act and react within our own fears – just as we can't help but act and react within our own ability to understand and feel love.

And that's the real problem: our awareness (or lack thereof). If we are unable to self-reflect and **to be honest with ourselves**, then we will be unable to recognize our own actions and reactions. If we can't recognize our own actions and reactions (and sometimes even when we do) it may be impossible to then change what we do, think or say – the choices we make.

The problem may be that we're simply afraid to be truly honest with ourselves. Admitting that we are reacting in fear is scarier than just ignoring it. And to be fair, it's difficult to recognize your own intentions (which is key to awareness) if you are just acting and reacting without removing the shroud of pretext.

Sally's comments, "*People have got to stop blaming their present on their past. You are who you are. If something's not working, just fix it. I can't stand when people aren't responsible for what they do"* now become far more complicated.

Emotional fight or flight is exactly what Sally is experiencing. Emotional fight or flight is the same kind of reaction we might have physiologically but within the expressive realm. We fight with judgment. We flight with denial. We find a way to feel superior while denying that we have any issues that might require self-reflection.

In other words, Sally is consciously unaware that she's afraid. Her physical symptoms, which haven't gone away over more than ten years, her emotional distance from anyone or anything that has molded her world, and her need to be in "better" control of her life (financially and otherwise) than others are indications that she is deeply insecure and afraid.

Now, when we look at Sally and see her being judgmental, irritated and acting in a way that some might consider inconsiderate, we see another person.

She says that people need to be responsible for the things that they say and do, and the whole time she's unaware that she isn't doing this very thing either. She is reacting just like the rest of us.

The difference for *us* now is that we understand her a little better. Can we find empathy though? Or are we going to travel down the same path Sally is walking? Will *we* now judge *her* by the standards *we* think are right? I think we probably will.

It's a vicious cycle!

Chapter Six
Kathy

Probably one of the most fascinating parts of this is that people irritate us. They get under our skin. We are easily annoyed by them. We think they should have done this or could have done that. We can't understand how they could possibly have come to the decisions that they did, married the people they married or hung out with the people they hung out with. Why didn't they have more sense? How many times have you thought or said the words, "He or she gets on my last nerve!" or "I can't believe he or she did or said that?"

What exactly is your last nerve? And why do people get on it?

Here's where honesty has to come into play once again or we will be unable have the opportunity for conscious awareness or true empathy.

If someone is getting on your nerves, you are most often describing a person who is causing you extreme irritation. It's difficult for us to imagine that the person who is grating on your nerves so badly is NOT the one with the problem. In order to stop the feelings of irritation, we have to stop feeling superior. Are we really better equipped to handle the situation? Are we really more intuitive? Are we smarter than he or she? Are we less able to get on other people's nerves than they are?

The funny thing is – we all do this. We all feel it. We all know people who we'd simply rather not be around because of some behavior they display or how they look or walk or dress or SOMETHING. We all become aggravated. It's a side-effect of being human and I'm not suggesting that we can erase that inherent part of our existence as people. That would be impossible. Perhaps it's not even a good idea. If we are here to learn anything, perhaps it is patience and good-will. One can't learn those things if they've never experienced the opposite. It's all about growing. Besides, we can only relate to what we know; and understand people through the experiences of our own lives.

My theory is, however, that if we are aware of why we feel the way we feel we can act more patiently, more kindly, more empathetically toward one another. The awareness of our actions and the reasons for them can be life-altering.

For instance, let's examine Sally's responses again. Sally can't stand her supervisor Kathy. There are many things about Kathy that get on Sally's nerves yet Sally has no choice but to interact with Kathy. She is being forced into a relationship with someone that she can't stand.

There are three ways to handle this. 1) She could react to her own feelings by being rude to Kathy, 2) She could avoid Kathy at all costs unless there's no choice and then swiftly avoid unnecessary conversation or eye contact or 3) She could find a way to accept Kathy's quirks and see past them.

Sally's already figured out the first two ways quite well. It's the third that eludes her. Interestingly, it's the third choice that would probably give her much more contented feelings.

Irritation is a negative response. Dislike, anger and impatience are too. When we feel those things, the reaction within ourselves is like a mirror image

– we feel even more negativity – we see things more negatively – we believe more negative things. The stress hormones that are released with pessimistic thinking are harmful to our physical selves and our emotional well-being. We are bringing ourselves down. We are bringing others down with us.

Not good.

If Sally can figure out a way to accept Kathy's quirks and see past them, then she would feel a level of understanding which might bring a certain amount of empathy to her heart. Empathy is simply about caring. Sally doesn't have to hang out with Kathy or have a personal relationship with her to care. She can care because Kathy is a human being. Sally can try to understand that Kathy's world has always been different than her own – that Kathy is loved – that Kathy is lovable – that Kathy deserves respect as much as Sally does. She doesn't have to like her – but it's possible to respect and honor her by assuming the best instead of seeing the worst.

The bottom line is that you don't have to agree with someone or something that they have done but you can attempt to try to understand where they're coming from.

These are theories that Sally may recognize as accurate but truly feeling them – standing in them – seeing Kathy (on every level) as equal – well, that's something else again.

So, how do we go about really seeing the people in our lives as equals? How do we walk a few steps in their moccasins?

We may need to look further than their physical appearance and differences that are so obvious – all the things that make us so unique that I spoke of in Chapters Three and Four. These things are important to understand, naturally. To recognize that no two people living or who have ever lived can see any situation in the same exact way is a gift of an opening heart.

However, in order to truly have an epiphany – a spark of empathy and understanding – to be truly "aware," we may need to look – not at what's different, but what between us is the same...

Chapter Seven
A Human Experience

So what about us *is* the same?
We are often not of the same race,
religion or culture. We are often not of
the same country or street. We are
often not the same gender. We don't
usually do the same job. We haven't
gone to the same schools nor had the
same teachers. We are not of the same
intelligence or have the same talents.
We didn't have the same parents and
even if we did, we aren't in the same
place within the family. Our life
experiences because of inborn
temperament and outward
circumstances can never be the same.
There are many, many differences
between us all. When you think about
it, it's really fascinating.

With all of those differences,
however, there is one thing that is
certain. We are human beings. Better
put by Dr. Wayne Dyer, "We are
spiritual beings having a human
experience."

A human experience. I like that.
Our experiences are different but we're
all having them. In other words, we're
having different experiences which

cause varying reactions but we are still human beings – sparks of energy (that some might call God), born into this world, at *this* time for a divine purpose. I believe that the purpose for human life is simply to understand what Love truly is.

A daunting task, for sure. Perhaps not one that most of us can attain completely – at least not within the human realm of duality.

So, is it about being able to stand firmly in what Love truly is all the time or is it just about being aware of what Love is all the time? I'm sure the real aspiration for Soul Itself is to stand in divine Love – to BE it. But, let's face it, in this human shell, with these emotions and memories, and reactions to our mental selves...we probably aren't going to be very successful most of the time.

Okay. Well, we can still be aware of it. And that awareness, if we are able to bring it into our hearts and remind ourselves all the time of it may well condition us to react to other people with a mind-frame of empathy.

We don't have to agree with the choices they make or like their personalities. We don't have to be overly nice to people who we have nothing in common with. We don't *have* to do anything.

But being aware that they are equal – the same – worthy – lovable – and more than anything – human - is a gift we not only give to them, but more than anything, we give it to ourselves.

People (including us, by the way) can only live in the process their lives have divulged to them. That's all we're doing, after all – speaking, acting, reacting and living within the limitations of our own lives.

If you are open to believing in reincarnation, then it would also be possible to assume that we are bringing past experiences into this present life as well. If that is your belief system, then there are a host of other reasons why a person might act as he or she does – working through the Karma of Soul.

Even without those beliefs, however, we can most assuredly see that each person, within his own frame of reference, dependant on his own experiences, culture, religion, society, gender, personality and many other dividing factors is practicing the art of living the best way they know how. Sure – we all make bad decisions. We all make good ones. We all act unkindly at times. We all know how to be nice.

The bottom line is - we all need and want to be loved.

So how do we go from knowing that in theory and acting like it in deed? How do we go from someone getting on our last nerve to (at the very least) accepting that whatever it is that we don't like about them has nothing to do with them at all (instead it's *our* problem). How do we empathize with who they are – even when there's no way of knowing why they are who they are? How do we stop making excuses for our judgments by continuing to judge them?

How do we turn it around?

Chapter Eight
Consciously Kind

Acceptance. Author, Arthur Gordon says that *"some people confuse acceptance with apathy, but there's all the difference in the world. Apathy fails to distinguish between what can and what cannot be helped; acceptance makes that distinction. Apathy paralyzes the will-to-action; acceptance frees it by relieving it of impossible burdens."*

In other words, in order to achieve empathy, understanding, and loving consciousness – in order to be able to accept people (including ourselves) for who we/they are – in order to react with kindness, patience and indulgence, we must first recognize that our awareness of the things that separate us can also be the bond that brings us closer.

Acceptance is about allowing people to be themselves. It's about being aware that we are capable of acting CONSICOUSLY kind.

After all, WE are no different than they are. We are human. That's it. We are not better. We are not smarter.

We don't deserve more than they do. If
we can open our hearts just a little we
can be the change we have so often
thought "they" should make.

Let's return one last time to Sally.
If Sally could see Kathy and others at
her place of work, as lovable people – if
she was able to reflect on the
similarities rather than the differences
– she would not need to like or enjoy
them necessarily, but she could be
aware; aware that they are just like
her. They simply express it differently.
They are living their lives as well as
they can. They are making decisions
from the wisest place in their own
hearts. They are fragile in their self-
esteem sometimes – just like she is.
They have strengths that are
comparable to hers. They love their
children. They pay their bills. They
enjoy time with loved ones.

The secret that allows the birth of
this awareness is simply listening to
what comes out of our own mouths.
REALLY listen to it! Listen to how we
speak to one another. And then (as we
speak it) we need to ask ourselves
"why?" We can justify it of course. We
can and we do.

But the end result is – no one deserves to be disrespected simply because we don't like the way they look or because we disagree with their choices, etc., etc., etc.

Once we actually realize that we are NOT superior – we are EQUAL – we are not better – we are the same; then we will not only hear what we say to people, we will begin to notice our own thoughts, and THAT is where awareness really begins to change us. It's all about being aware of **our thoughts**; not JUST what we DO but what we THINK.

Changing our thoughts is not an easy thing. After all, we are creatures of our own lives, our environment and our own conditioned responses. We should probably assume that we can't completely change every internal thing about ourselves. In fact, for reasons of growth, it's probably not a good idea that we become "perfect" (not that something like that is even possible).

But being aware of our thoughts allows us to make the choice – the conscious choice – to not say things that are unkind – to not do things that are hurtful.

What we often fail to appreciate is that **thought comes before action and intent.** We think it, we make a choice, and we either ignore or accept our own intentions and then we act. This happens in seconds. To change actions, we need to be honest about our intentions, we need to realize our choice and first and foremost, we need to be mindful of our own thoughts as they sneak into our consciousness.

After a while, the deep realization that we can't understand anyone else – that we can barely understand ourselves creates the fertile ground for the expression of divine Love.

Divine Love.

According to Daniel B. Holeman, *"Pure Divine Love is what we all are. Regardless of appearances and behaviors, each sentient Being's existence springs from the core of Love.*[6]

Empathy is always an option of consciousness. For awareness to become the key, we must open our hearts – not our heads.

---

[6] Celestial Heart © Daniel B. Holeman, AwakenVisions.com

A Perfect Seed

Deep inside me there laid a seed.
For many years that seed was me.
Its roots imbedded deep inside
did hunger for a brighter light.
And as the tides of time were passed
the seed inside was meant to last.
And one bright day; One Autumn night
it rose within to gain new sight.

As Spirit touched it like a rain
it filled with passion and with pain
but still it grew to lofty heights
and burned an incandescence light
that soon had filled my every pore.
It seized the seed I was before
and turned it into what might be
that grows inside from perfect seeds.

And now I blossom deep within
where seeds are sown and soon begin
to bring themselves into the light
that burns and sings with true delight.
I walk in wonder as I grow.
All through me an expanding flow
of all that I could ever be
is born from such a perfect seed.

-Anne Jobes

Read Anne's other books:

Powerless —

Healing From the Addiction of a Loved One

Love is What's Left

The Trickle of Time

Sheena

Spirits of the Heart · Volume One

Spirits of the Heart · Volume Two

Spirits of the Heart · Volume Three

Of Light and Sound

Journey of the Heart · Volume One

Journey of the Heart · Volume Two

Melancholy Moments